Pebble®

My World

Communities
in My World

by Ella Cane

Consulting Editor: Gail Saunders-Smith, PhD

CAPSTONE PRESS
a capstone imprint

Pebble Books are published by Capstone Press,
1710 Roe Crest Drive, North Mankato, Minnesota 56003
www.capstonepub.com

Library of Congress Cataloging-in-Publication Data
Cane, Ella.
Communities in my world / by Ella Cane.
pages cm. — (Pebble books. My world)
Includes index.
Audience: K to Grade 3.
ISBN 978-1-4765-3120-5 (library binding)
ISBN 978-1-4765-3462-6 (paperback)
ISBN 978-1-4765-3468-8 (ebook pdf)
1. Communities—Juvenile literature. 2. City and town life—Juvenile literature.
3. Country life—Juvenile literature. I. Title.
HT152.C357 2014
307—dc23   2013005894

Summary: Simple text and full-color photographs introduce different kinds of
communities to the reader.

Note to Parents and Teachers
The My World set supports national curriculum standards
for social studies related to people, places, and environments.
This book describes and illustrates communities. The images
support early readers in understanding the text. The repetition
of words and phrases helps early readers learn new words.
This book also introduces early readers to subject-specific
vocabulary words, which are defined in the Glossary section.
Early readers may need assistance to read some words and to
use the Table of Contents, Glossary, Read More, Internet Sites,
and Index sections of the book.

Printed in the United States   5517

Table of Contents

What Is a Community?

Look around you.

Who and what do you see?

Your community!

A community is a place

where people live together.

Rural Communities

Rural communities are
quiet places.
Homes are usually
far apart.

There are many farms in rural communities. Rachel and her family live on a farm with horses.

There are few people
in a rural community.
Lia has 10 children
in her class at school.

Urban Communities

Devin lives in an urban community. His apartment in the city sits high above the busy streets below.

When Devin and
his mom want pizza,
they can choose from
many restaurants.

Suburban Communities

Maya lives in a suburb. The houses on her street all look the same.

Maya walks to school
with her neighbors.
After school,
she plays with friends
at the park.

A community is made up
of people and places.
What's your community like?

Glossary

community—a place where people live together

neighbor—a person who lives near or next door to the person speaking

restaurant—a place where people pay to eat

rural—away from cities and towns

suburb—a community near a city

suburban—having to do with a town or village very close to a city

urban—having to do with a city

Read More

Leake, Diyan. *Teachers.* People In the Community. Chicago: Heinemann Library, 2008.

Robertson, J. Jean. *My Community.* Little World Social Studies. Vero Beach, Fla.: Rourke Pub., 2011.

Tourville, Amanda Doering. *Whose Gear Is This?* Community Helper Mysteries. Mankato, Minn.: Capstone Press, 2012.

Internet Sites

FactHound offers a safe, fun way to find Internet sites related to this book. All of the sites on FactHound have been researched by our staff.

Here's all you do:

Visit *www.facthound.com*

Type in this code: 9781476531205

Check out projects, games and lots more at
www.capstonekids.com

Index

Word Count: 138
Grade: 1
Early-Intervention Level: 15

Editorial Credits
Shelly Lyons, editor; Juliette Peters, designer; Marcie Spence, media researcher;
Eric Manske, production specialist

Photo Credits
Alamy Images: Jim West, 20; iStockphoto: bonniej, 18, nullplus, 14; Newscom:
Frances M. Roberts, 10; Shutterstock: Dustie, 16, Elena Elisseeva, 1, gorillaimages,
8, maxstockphoto, cover (top), MaxyM, 6, Pablo Scapinachis, cover (bottom), Rob
Marmion, 4, Zholobov Vadim, 12